AF380337

DON'T BE A! BE AN A!

The 9 requirements to stop being <u>A</u> participant and become <u>THE</u> leader.

By Jake Bollig

Be sure to read other books by
Jake Bollig including:

Gifts From Nicholas

Available at every major online or retail outlet

For more information about Jake Bollig,

Including hiring him for a speaking or training event

Contact via email at questions@jakebollig.com

Or visit his website: JakeBollig.com

Anom Aly Publishing Company

4 NE 10th St. #262

Oklahoma City, OK 73104

First Edition: November 2017

The publisher is not responsible for websites (or their content) that are not owned by the publisher.

Cover Art: Jeff Bowman

ISBN 978-0-9995997-0-9 (Hardback)

LCCN 2017917337

Printed in the United States of America

For information about hiring Mr. Bollig to speak at an event, send inquiry to

questions@jakebollig.com

<u>Definition of THE</u>: Devoting one or more people or things already mentioned or **assumed to be common knowledge.**

<u>Definition of A</u>: Used to indicate membership of a class of people or things.

Interpretation

A <u>THE</u> stands above all others.

An "<u>a</u>" is a part of the crowd.

You get to decide what you want to be.

Let's go.

Contents

Intro

Requirement 1: Compare you to you

1

Requirement 2: Be a pro

7

Requirement 3: Fail big

15

Requirement 4: Embrace the pain

21

Requirement 5: Think Universally

31

Requirement 6: Commit

40

Requirement 7: Edison muffs

49

Requirement 8: In the flow

57

Requirement 9: Be THE now

65

Conclusion

74

Eight quotes

76

Daily reminders to cut out

92

Contact Jake for programs

99

Acknowledgments

Depending on how you look at it, this book was written in a few days or it was written over 38 years.

I must believe that it was written as a compilation of lessons I have learned throughout my life and the words chose to come out now.

I must thank my parents for their eternal support. It has been a journey for the ages and I couldn't ask for better support.

Thank you to all the coaches I had in my young athletic life that taught me so much. I now understand and utilize many of the lessons.

I want to thank all the people in this world who have spent their lives being kind, courageous and lifting others up. Without people helping others this world would be a dramatically different experience.

I especially want to thank two wonderful ladies in my life, Alysia and Paityn. Without the support of these beautiful souls this book would not be a reality. I am eternally grateful.

Introduction

I wrote this book for myself to solve a problem I had been dealing with for a large part of my life. I needed a shift in my mindset. I needed to change the way I was thinking about myself and my contributions to the world.

I consider myself to be a hard worker, one who takes pride in setting goals and accomplishing them. Do you consider yourself to have the same type of mentality?

I'm sure, since you are reading this, you have a desire to improve upon yourself just as I did when I wrote it.

For me, I felt as though it didn't matter how much work I put in, I was never having the success I thought I truly deserved.

I read the books, I created the good habits, I studied people who have had success in different fields, I maintained a healthy diet and overall thought I was doing the steps necessary to be "successful" but I never felt like I was truly exploding into my potential.

Does this sound like anything you have ever dealt with? Are you dealing with a little bit of those thoughts right now? Maybe you are having a large dose of those thoughts right now.

I knew that it must be something simple, because complexity, in my mind, is never a good answer. And when I uncovered it, it was, and is, actually very simple.

The following statement is not an arrogant statement, it's a mindset shift that I hope you'll experience by the time you finish this book.

By the time you finish this sentence, it is very likely that I will have already completed writing several more books. Why do I tell you that?

The reason I tell you that is because I made a shift in my thinking that allowed me to create those additional books and that is what we are going to talk about.

You will learn all you need to know about shifting from being <u>a</u> participant to be <u>THE</u> leader. It is so simple yet so profound that many people will get more than their money's worth, from this book, simply by hearing the title.

Other books want you to read all the way through before telling you "the secret", however, I want you to get the value up front and right away.

Here it is.

The reason I will have written several more books by the time you have read this is because I made the decision that I am no longer going to be **an** author, I am going to be **THE** author.

That's it.

It's a simple yet very profound shift in the way

you do everything in life. The 9 requirements, I made for myself will hopefully help you understand the psyche behind it, and you are about to make the same shift (if you haven't already).

This is not about boasting, bragging or arrogance. It's about a mindset to expect the best from yourself and get the most of your own potential.

You are no longer a manager, an employee, an entrepreneur, a model, an actor, an actress, a real estate investor, an artist, a musician or a parent.

You must make the shift to being THE manager, THE employee, THE entrepreneur, THE model, THE actor, THE actress, THE real estate investor, THE artist, THE musician or THE parent!

Does this make sense to you? Be THE. DON'T BE AN a.

Let's try a short mental exercise.

Visualize yourself being **a participant** in a very important 5K race of your choosing. Take 10 seconds and visualize yourself. How are others treating you? How confident do you feel? Do you fit in or stand out? Do others expect you to succeed or do you blend in with everyone else?

Now visualize yourself entering the same race as **THE** participant. The person that everyone turns to look at when you enter the race. Visualize this for 10 seconds.

Do you feel more confident? What is your posture like? Are you worried or courageous?

"A" participant would go through the motions of the race, whereas THE participant would go to the race with a purpose.

You want to be the person that people think of when they need your skill.

If you're in acting and someone needs a role field, you want them to think, "I need THE actor ______."

If you're into entrepreneurship and someone needs advice you want them to think of THE entrepreneur. YOU.

If you work for a company, and a tough assignment comes up, you want them to think of THE employee for the job. YOU.

Be the first person that people think of when they think of your expertise.

Try this short exercise for a mind shift. Fill in the blanks:

I am not a/an ______________________, I am THE ______________________.

Now, let's get started.

DISCLAIMER: If at this point in your life, you do not want to be known as THE in your field of choice then I urge you to stop reading. From this point on in the book the material assumes that only those who want to be known as THE are reading and the context is important.

If you are still not sure if you want to just be a part of the crowd or make the decision to be a THE then you are not ready for the rest of the material in this book. I respect your decision and I understand. But, if that is you then please put this book down now.

If you have made the decision to be THE and not be an A, then follow me. We have work to do.

***If you are a manager, business owner, or organizer, this book format was made for you. It can be read quickly, so you can share the book with your groups and have a meeting about it the next day.**

<u>Hire Jake</u> to speak at your next
event or corporate training.

Send inquiry to

questions@JakeBollig.com

Requirement 1

Compare you to you

A's compare themselves to other people, not THE's. THE's are the measuring stick for others, and you aren't a participant in the comparison-with-others game. Your only involvement in that game is from the front.

Requirement 1:
Compare you to you

Measure against yourself

Requirement number 1 states that you must compare you to you. Society wants you to compare yourself to your neighbor. Why in the world would you compare yourself to your neighbor when you are two completely different people? And your neighbor shouldn't think twice about comparing themselves to you.

An "a" compares themselves to their neighbor because they are looking for social validation of their presence in life, a THE compares themselves to the best they can possibly do.

If you are THE, then comparing yourself to someone else would mean that your models of success would actually be bringing you down and not lifting you up.

You will know, when you lay in bed at night, because you will fall asleep quickly, if you gave everything you had that day. Here is a clue: If it takes you 20 minutes to fall asleep every night then you are probably comparing yourself to others instead of comparing yourself to your potential.

A THE doesn't "go to bed", they fall asleep because they have nothing left to give that day.

Does this sound ridiculous?

It's not.

You must only compare yourself to your potential and guess what... your potential never ends.

Next.

Failure or success do not affect your capabilities

Is it important if others succeed or fail? Is it important if you succeed or fail? Context is important because your success or failure has no bearing on your ability or capabilities. You are what you are at that moment.

If you are racing against someone, the results of the race have no impact on your ability. If you win the race your ability in that moment will be the same as if you would have lost the race. Your duty is to compare you to you and make any adjustments needed to improve, and be THE.

An "a" would assess their abilities based on the results of the race. What if the person you were racing had a pulled hamstring and couldn't run fast that day? Does that mean you are better after the race than before it started because you won the race?

The victory may give you a trophy, it may be a way to measure yourself socially but it has no impact on your actual abilities.

You must understand that your own standards should be far greater than any stipulation that society would be able to offer.

An "a" looks for the social validation to prove their worth. But THE know that social validation is simply a by-product or ancillary circumstance from having the mindset of becoming THE.

Your capabilities are amazing

Your abilities are truly amazing, but you are underutilizing them. You know that you are leaving gas in the potential-tank. You were not gifted the tools you have just to leave them hanging in the garage in their plastic wrapping.

Stop being afraid of putting your tools out into the world. Who cares what others think? If you try something 100 times and it doesn't work yet, ask yourself if the task is worth it. If your answer is yes then continue, if it is not then make a change.

Make sure your answer comes from you and not social pressures that you succumb to.

This is not a positive affirmation talk, this is real talk. If you can read this then you can use your eyes to interpret the world and the gifts you can offer it.

Compare you to you

Many people in this world do not have the ability to see and are still producing far more than many others with the gift of sight. And that includes you.

No disrespect, I say this with all respect and sincerity, but how is it possible that someone without the gift of vision is producing more value for this world than you are?

How is it possible that a person born without legs or arms is able to provide massive value and inspiration to people all around the world and you are afraid to deliver your message to the masses?

You must realize the gifts you have available to you at this very moment. You have everything you need to leave the "a" world behind and be a THE.

Don't be an A!

Be THE.

Next.

Applying the requirement:
Compare you to you.

1. The first key to change is to recognize what needs to be changed. Be honest with yourself and list who you are currently comparing yourself to.

2. Think of a few instances in which you have either won or lost lately. For example: a contract at work, an audition, a new client, a promotion, or an award. What did you learn from those experiences regardless of whether you won or lost?

3. Often, if we are thinking like an "a" and not "THE" we find reasons we can't do something instead of reasons that we can. Think of an obstacle you are facing right now and reaffirm, with three reasons, why you are capable of overcoming the challenge.

Requirement 2

Be a pro

Definition of
professional:
Person of extreme
competence or highly
skilled in a certain way

Requirement 2: Be a Pro

The pro goes to work

Requirement number 2 states that THE pro goes to work when it's the last thing they want to do. When they are sick they go to work. When they are sad they go to work. When they stayed up too late the night before they go to work. THE professional goes to work when others wouldn't.

That's what makes you a pro.

The pro doesn't allow a bunch of time to go by before acting on their duties. The pro knows that too much time is the enemy of progress.

The pro goes to work.

The pro goes to work when they've been working for 15 hours and just remembered they didn't put in their daily writing because of crazy circumstances. For most people, this would be a justifiable excuse to put off the writing until tomorrow. They would say, "It's okay if I miss just one day."

But it's not okay.

The pro pulls themselves off the couch, bed, chair, floor and they force themselves to get in their writing or whatever daily habit they forgot to do.

The pro shows up.

You are a pro. You won't see an "a" put in the work day in and day out. And you don't want to be an "a".

You are THE.

<u>THE</u> best in class doesn't make excuses for themselves and neither will you.

Take satisfaction in knowing that you are disciplined enough to work when it's the last thing you want to do. You know this will breed unstoppable confidence.

Make the actions necessary.

Go. To. Work.

Next.

Discipline

The pro has an incredible amount of discipline. Discipline is defined as – *the practice of training people to obey rules or a code of behavior, using punishment to correct disobedience.*

You set the rules of your discipline. Your punishment for failure in discipline is total dissatisfaction with yourself.

You set the rules you intend to play by, the code of behavior which you know will lead you closest to the realization of your full potential. A pro sets the standard, their own personal standard. And to break that standard isn't a letdown of someone else, it's a disappointment in themselves.

You are a pro. What is the discipline you have set for yourself? Have you reviewed it every day to insure you're following your rules? Are you strict like a <u>THE</u> should be or do you cheat like an "<u>a</u>"?

The punishment administered to a pro is mental punishment. It's the feeling of knowing they didn't give their best effort. Be disciplined. You must give your best effort and be disciplined. Not for anyone else's benefit, but for the benefit of knowing when you lay your head down at night that you did everything within your ability to move the needle forward.

The punishment of not being disciplined like a pro is a clouded mind when you go to sleep. The punishment is a guilty conscious for knowing you're not giving 100%. The punishment is when people ask you what you do and they should already know what you do because you're a "THE", not an "a".

Be disciplined.

If you're not satisfied with your discipline, then you're thinking of it right now. What should you be more disciplined in right now? Is it your diet? Is it the amount of work you put in? Are you slacking off when you know you should be working? You know what it is.

Be disciplined.

Discomfort is your friend

The pro knows the value of discomfort. Why are you avoiding discomfort? Why aren't you looking at discomfort as a necessary aspect of growth? The pro looks at discomfort and says "Let's do this!" Is that what you say?

You must seek out the daily discomforts and accept them. Don't waste time thinking about how you don't want to do the task. Just do the task.

An "a" looks for ways, avenues or shortcuts around the discomfort. An "a" looks for someone else to handle the discomfort. An "a" doesn't have the stones necessary to take on the discomfort so the "a" just sits and grovels in their own little misery.

What discomfort are you avoiding right this moment? What is it? Is it a project you are procrastinating on? Is it a script you've been talking about writing for 5 years, but are too scared of what people will say? Is it taking your project door-to-door to spread the word about it, but you're too scared of rejection?

Guess what? Everyone is scared at first. But "THE's" do something about it. They work through the discomfort knowing that a valuable lesson, growth or gain is awaiting just on the other side.

You need to put this book down right now and make action on some discomfort you're avoiding. Do it.

Be a Pro

Take five minutes to put an action step
together towards something you're avoiding.
Send an email to ask about a meeting, make
a phone call you've been putting off or ask an
expert a question about your industry that you
need to know.

Do it now. I'll be here when you get back.
Send the email, deliver the text message,
make the call or whatever it is you need to do
to make action on a discomfort you're avoiding.

When you're done, move on to the next
chapter.

Don't be an A!

Be THE!

Next.

Applying the requirement:
Be a Pro

1. What must you do to shift your habits to that of a pro? If you already are a pro, then you know improvements can be made. What area of your life do you need to be a pro in?

2.What discipline should you be focusing on? What discipline will you commit to focusing on for the next 7 days minimum?

3.What discomfort are you avoiding? What is one step you can take to conquer that discomfort?

***If you want Jake to speak to your organization, send an email to**

questions@JakeBollig.com

Requirement 3

Fail Big

Definition of fail: a grade that
is not high enough to pass an
examination or test
Definition of big: of considerable
size, extent, or intensity

Requirement 3:
Fail Big

Risk your time

Requirement number 3 states that you must be willing to risk your time for the chance at achievement.

An "a" is unwilling to risk their time because they are afraid on missing out in some other area. They just end up not doing anything resembling mastery and coast into the end of life disappointed at all the wasted time.

Don't be an a.

A THE is willing to risk their time for something they believe in. A THE understands that truly great things, that come from this life, take an investment in time and you're not getting that time back.

An a says "I don't have time to do _______". A THE says, "if it's worth it, I'll make time for it." And if it's not worth it, the THE doesn't waste time on anymore thought about it.

An "a" listens to people around them that ask, "Why are you working so hard on that when you're not even getting paid?" That statement can destroy the concentration of the "a".

But not a THE. A THE pays that question no

mind and it doesn't affect them because they have a vision which can't be broken. They give zero attention to people who don't understand it.

Be willing to miss the "big game" on Saturday in pursuit of a vision, dream or goal. All of your friends may be attending the game, and it may be the biggest game of the year, but that does not matter.

An "a" would attend the game and put their dreams off for another day. A THE would willingly risk missing out on a great game, and instead, opt for the possibility of making their dreams a reality.

Be willing to risk your time and be willing to live with it if it doesn't work out the way you originally intended. A THE trusts themselves regardless of the outcome.

Don't be an a.

Be THE.

Risk your reputation

Are you willing to put your reputation on the line for what you believe in? Are you accepting of the social opinions if your ideas fall flat in society? Do you have what it takes inside to make a stand for your beliefs, even if they won't be popular?

Before acting on an idea, an "a" worries about

what their co-workers, industry, friends or associates will think about them.

A THE person believes in themselves and are willing to risk their reputation amongst their peers if it's for something they believe in. A THE has a strong moral compass and therefore trusts in themselves regardless of the outcome.

Are you living like an "a" or a THE?

Many people fail to provide for their family because of fear that their peers will "make fun of" their means of providing. For many, their pride gets in the way of their progress.

This is not you though. You are committed to doing what it takes. And you are committed to doing it in a big way!

Be willing to risk your reputation.

Listen to your future self

Your intuition matters. Your instincts are more correct than you give them credit for. The more work you put in, the better your instincts become.

Are you trusting your gut, or are you doing things for your mind? Are you playing it safe because you feel secure or are you taking calculated risks because you know the upside is far greater by going big?

Is your future self going to be more proud of

you paying off the bill on time, or taking a shot at finishing the script and sending it into a publishing house?

When you're on a porch swing at 80 years old, are you going to be more proud that you attempted to learn public speaking or that you decided not to because you didn't want to be embarrassed?

An "a" worries about little things that don't matter such as what their friends will think about their new business.

A <u>THE</u> listens to their future self and understands they must do the thing because it's necessary, not because someone else approves or disapproves.

What have you been pondering lately that you can apply the porch swing test to? What advice would your 80-year-old-self give you? How does your gut feel about your decision? What do you see happening?

No decision worth making is ever going to be 100%. You will be wrong sometimes and that's okay. In the end, you must trust yourself and your ability to make decisions.

An "a" makes a decision and worries.

A <u>THE</u> makes a decision and <u>has faith</u>.

Applying the Requirement: Fail Big

1.An "a" would rather attend extracurricular activities instead of risking that time on their dreams. What are you spending too much time on right now that's taking away from the goals you want to achieve?

2.What area of your life are you holding back in because you are worried about what your co-workers, neighbors, friends, relatives or social media followers will think? Once you identify it, make the decision to reverse the thinking you currently have.

3. What area of your life do you feel you are not listening to your instincts? Which area, can you see, needs improvement but your mind tells you to overlook it? Can you identify an area of your life or career that your future self will be disappointed about if you don't change?

Requirement 4

Embrace the pain

Embrace the pain on your journey. Don't expect pain to come but anticipate it might. It may show up, and when it does, stand up and own it.

Requirement 4

Embrace the pain

The power of habits

Requirement number 4 states that a THE masters their habits. An "a" is <u>inconsistent</u> with their habits, a THE knows that habits are the key to success.

Why does the "a" shy away from good habits? Why would you avoid the very thing that you know is good for you? Why don't you do more of the daily quality actions that bring success and avoid the detrimental daily doings that cultivate your destruction?

Are you afraid of the pain?

Do you avoid the good habits because you feel they are not worth it, because you don't want to put your body through the pain, or maybe you have simply slacked off lately?

It doesn't always have to be physical pain you go through. Most of the time it isn't physical pain. 90% of the time you are avoiding the mental pain of change.

You are a creature of comfort. Your desire to

live in a state of comfort will breed unhealthy habits. You think that everything is good at a certain level.

A THE performer understands that pain is a normal occurrence with their habits.

Why is it important to embrace the pain, own the pain and conquer the pain? It's important because many of the best rewards in life are on the other side of it.

A great bicep is on the other side of intense and painful workouts in the gym. Great innovations are on the other side of migraine headaches and countless nights in front of a whiteboard mapping out a solution. The greatest gift in the world, the birth of a child is on the other side of the intensity and immense pain many women experience during child birth.

Think about that last one for a minute. The greatest creation on this planet is welcomed to this world just seconds after one of the most painful experiences on this planet.

When it seems to be to hard to finish or you feel like giving up then you are probably exactly where you need to be. If you see the outcome in your mind then do whatever it takes to get through the pain.

The pain can be mental pain of trying to come

up with the creative strategy for your business or the pain of a relationship breaking into pieces.

The pain comes in many forms. Embrace it.

Remember this question when dealing with immense pain: What about this moment could alter my direction to make this the greatest thing that's happened to me?

An "a" personality tries to avoid the pain, and thus they never achieve their highest potential.

A THE knows the pain is coming and accepts it as part of the journey. The daily positive habits that push you, are the most important of your daily habits.

Be a THE and face those daily disciplines with courage.

The pain of defeat

The time of defeat is not the time to feel sorry for yourself. Defeat is not some universal permission slip to look for sympathy. Defeat is a tool to let you know exactly where you stand in the order of things.

Where do you stand right now? What defeat have you recently suffered? How are you going to use the defeat as a measuring stick for your next move?

Is it fun to suffer defeat? Absolutely not. Is it enjoyable to see projects you work on fail miserably? Nope. Do you like to commit all of your time and not get the payback you expected? Of course you don't.

Who cares?

Nobody cares.

A great coach once said, "90% of the people don't care when something bad happens to you and the other 10% are glad it happened to you."

You only have two jobs when suffering a great defeat. The first is to figure out the lesson in the experience so you can hopefully not repeat it again. The second job you have is to remember the defeat and somehow use it as fuel to propel you forward in your pursuit of your potential.

That's it.

Your job is not to sulk, whine, look for sympathy, post about it on social media or any other selfish form of attention gathering. Those are the actions an "a" will take.

A THE does the two steps mentioned. A THE looks for the lesson and then uses the experience to propel them forward.

How are you using a defeat you've recently suffered? Is it robbing you of energy or is it energizing you?

Did a relationship end, a business fail, a project crash? Did you lose money, stop going to the gym or miss out on a publishing deal? It doesn't matter.

The thing that matters is that you handle your defeats like THE leader, THE general, THE commander of your own personal mission.

Don't be an A!

Embrace your defeats and move on.

The pain of regret

What do you regret? Think about it, what are some of the biggest regrets in your life?

You probably came up with some painful stuff, maybe some things you haven't thought about in a very long time. You may have even recalled some events that you wanted to forget completely. Did you come up with anything that you would rather not think about?

Good.

Now that you have created a bonfire of feelings within your mind, you can use those emotions for good.

It's time to take those regrets and make them the best thing that's ever happened to you. You must use the energy that exists in that pain to go do good in the world.

You cannot change the moment that you regret but you can choose to view it in a completely different way. You can make the decision that your regrets will only empower you and were meant to happen, so you can share a gift with the world.

If you didn't tell someone you loved them enough, then use that as energy to make sure you let everyone you care about know how much you love them.

If you did a bad job managing people at work in the past, then use that as a lesson that you will go out of your way to be the best manager you can be.

If you didn't give 100% effort on a project, sport or business and it failed, use that as fuel to always insure that effort will never be a deciding factor in future outcomes, because you will always give your best.

An "a" looks at regrets and lives in the past. An "a" looks for reasons why the regrets are the

Embrace the Pain

worst thing that's ever happened to them.

A THE still feels the emotion of the regret but chooses to use it as a positive defining moment in their life, even if the moment was extremely painful.

Do not try to hide from the pain of your regret, instead, use the pain as fuel for the good you can do for this world.

Don't be an A and dwell in the regrets with self-pity.

Be THE and use those regrets as a force for good.

Next.

Applying the Requirement:

Embrace the pain

1. What habit are you avoiding that you know you should be doing? Commit the next 7 days to rebuilding this habit.

2. What recent defeat is causing you to lose focus? It can be in a relationship of any kind, a project, a contract awarded to another company. What lesson can you take from it, so that you may get the value and let the bad energy go?

3. Make a commitment to yourself that your past regrets will now become fuel for your future actions. Your past is not an indicator of who you are right now in this moment. Apply the energy from those regrets as a force for good in this world.

Requirement 5

Think universally

Once you understand your role in the universe you cease to worry about things that don't matter.

Requirement 5

Think Universally

Focus on what matters

Clothes don't matter. Cars don't matter. Homes don't matter.

What matters?

Progress matters.

Focus on what's important and what's important is progress. When are you in your most fulfilled state of mind? When do you feel most accomplished? What is the most internally rewarding feeling?

Is it when you buy a new car? How about when you purchase a new suit, is that your most rewarding time? Those are both fun experiences, but the material purchases don't take you closer to your potential and therefore aren't the goal of a THE.

Are those purchases and experiences fun? Absolutely. Should you continue to experience those aspects of life? If you choose then I certainly can't see anything wrong with it.

The difference is an "a" often defines

themselves by those material possessions or experiences where as a THE knows the little secret that those things won't lead to fulfillment.

I say get as much of everything as you can and give as much of everything as you can. Just make sure and understand where those things fit on the hierarchy of your path.

Regarding the material desires:

A THE is grateful.

A THE is appreciative.

A THE is generous.

But the THE is not fooled into believing the material desires are anything more than what they are. An experience. Status does not matter. Popularity does not matter.

The quest is what matters in the end and that is where the main focus is.

Abundance is everywhere,

look for it

A THE sees an abundant world, filled with resources and possibilities. An "a" maintains a scarcity mindset and doesn't believe enough exists for them.

You must see an abundance in this world. You

have a never-ending supply of creativity inside of you, you literally cannot run out of it unless you cease to exist on this planet.

Are you operating with a mentality of endless creativity to achieve your outcomes or are you looking for reasons you can't achieve your potential?

Are you limiting your potential because you're playing it safe? How do you set your quota at work? Is it based on what you believe, someone else's opinion or past experiences?

If someone in the organization says you should have 10% growth, you should ask them, what's keeping it from 100% growth.

Too often we set quotas in our lives based on someone else's performance. An "a" says, "The competition did 10% growth, so we should try to do 12%."

The industry standard is not your standard. You set the standard for yourself. Do this in every area of your life and no end can be placed on the amount of abundance you will see.

It takes the same amount of energy to think small as it does to think abundantly. The only reason you won't think abundantly is because you're afraid to get uncomfortable.

It may take days, months or years to realize the visions. Don't get caught up in the instant gratification of small goals. Get energized and passionate about the pursuit of the massive abundant living that you are meant to do.

An "a" lives with a scarcity mindset.

A THE knows this universe is abundant.

Don't be an A!

Be kind

Definition of kind: *having or showing a friendly, generous, and considerate nature.*

Don't wait for others to be kind to you, be the catalyst of kindness.

An "a" operates with a selfish mindset and expects others to say the first word. A THE offers up the compliment, holds the door without expectation of a thank you, and says hi to the elderly person eating by themselves at the restaurant.

Be kind because it's the character of person you are and choose to be. Don't be kind because you think it will get you favors in the future. This is kindness with the wrong intention.

Think of your kindness as the start of a great chain of events. Each time you display kindness it could set in motion a chain of life-altering positive events for someone you don't even personally know or have ever met.

Be kind because you choose to.

An "a" expects something in return for their

kindness. They think their acts will benefit them, this makes the act a selfish one.

A THE knows the act will be a benefit to them because the energy behind the action is with a pure heart.

Have you ever held the door for someone and then become disappointed they didn't respond with a "thank you?" This is an example of the kindness an "a" demonstrates. Don't let someone's response to your action dictate your opinion.

A THE is kind because, in most situations, it's simply the right way to be.

Be kind like a THE is.

Don't be an A!

*I understand that some situations arise where, for the safety of persons or property, kindness cannot be demonstrated.

Applying the requirement:
Think Universally

1. Today you'll make the decision to shift your focus to the importance things that have the largest impact in your life. You choose to not allow inconveniences to distract you from your main objective.

2. What areas of your life do you see scarcity and lack? You must identify and shift your thinking because you understand there are no limits to your creativity. And as long as you have creativity then you have access to the abundance of this world.

3. What areas of your life can you demonstrate more kindness? Make it a point to seek out opportunities to be kind, because you know the acts will be transmitted to the others around you. Do this without expectation of favors or acts of kindness in return

Think Universally

Requirement 6:

Commit

You must remind yourself daily of your commitment. An 'a" is afraid of commitment, they are scared that they could be wrong. A THE commits fully and focuses on doing the best they can.

Commit

Requirement 6:
Commit

Overcommit

The 6th requirement states you must commit. And to take it one level higher, anyone who is a THE overcommits.

Are you afraid of overcommitting? Why are you afraid of overcommitting? The overcommitted are the ones confident enough to rule their world.

People say under commit and over deliver, but that is a terrible philosophy and should be discarded immediately! Why? Because the people at the top do both, they overcommit AND overdeliver.

What does overcommitting look like? It looks like you agreeing to a challenge that others are too scared to accept. It looks like you forcing yourself to put the work in even though your friends are going to the lake all weekend. It looks like the roadmap to being "THE" and leaving the world of "a's" behind you.

Why are you playing it safe? What are you scared of? Are you scared to ruffle a few feathers of those people around you? Overcommit and make others believe in your vision and you have nothing to worry about.

Commit

What happens when you overcommit and overdeliver a few times? What do you think will happen? You'll have the reputation of the person that can do the extraordinary. It's not rocket science. It's simply making the commitment to give more effort than anyone else can possibly imagine.

You must overcommit and overdeliver. You have the skills necessary to do this. What does it take? All it takes is the mindset to do so. You are more than strong enough to accomplish this task. Are you up for this task?

OVERCOMMIT!

What will your rewards be? Your rewards will be many, one of which is a sound nights' sleep knowing you're executing on your potential. A THE isn't afraid to overcommit.

Take a minute to hear someone saying the following, fill your name in where the blanks are: "_______________ overcommits every time and always overdelivers, that's why _________________ is THE person to go to for _____________________."

1% is too much of a chance

Are you 99% committed or 100%? What's the difference? Obviously, the difference is 1%, but the bigger difference is the ever so slight chance that you will be distracted. 1% leaves room for you to sabotage your potential. Your being distracted will keep you in the "a" category and prevent you from being **THE**.

Do you want to lose everything you've worked for because you can't commit the extra 1%? What does it matter? Isn't the 99% commitment good enough? It is good enough if you want to be considered a simple "a". It is good enough if you want to bid against 4 other people for a job, contract or role. 99% is good enough if you want to live a great life. Except you're not in this to live "a" great life, you're in this to live "THE" great life!

You are blessed with the tools, talents and knowledge needed to max out your potential, but nothing can be maxed out at 99%.

99% is saying it's okay to eat one potato chip. 99% is believing that you work harder than everyone else but you don't. 99% leaves just enough room for someone to sneak by you at the finish line and snatch away your dreams in an instant.

You are 100% committed. Let the "a's" be 99% committed. It's okay to be 99%, and there's nothing wrong with it. Except it's not the way you choose to live your life.

You are 100% committed.

Be 100% committed.

Be **THE**.

Die for the truth

You must be willing to give up everything for the truth. In the end, the truth matters. Don't get caught up in thinking that you are going to live forever on Earth. It's not going to happen. Be willing to die for what you believe to be your core truth.

If you are scared, if you hesitate or if you enter the game without being committed and confident then you will lose. You may not lose immediately, you may get a lucky win. But in the long run you will lose.

Commit with the mentality of a hero and carry that mentality with you in your task.

What are you willing to die for? Are you willing to push yourself in your craft? Are you willing to see how far you can go? Are you willing to set far-reaching goals and commit without knowing how to accomplish them?

Commit!

You better be willing to put in the work, the reading, the workouts, the overtime, the long days, the sleepless nights and the hours on end without eating if that's what it takes.

Remind yourself right now (FILL IN THE BLANK): I am known for my relentless work ethic and my willingness to outwork everyone because I am THE ___________________.
I am not just "A" ______________ like so many others settle for. I am THE

_________________________ and I back it up
with my persistence, relentlessness and
COMMITMENT!

*to bring this workshop to your company, send
an inquiry to questions@jakebollig.com

Applying the 6th requirement:

Commit

1. What am I willing to overcommit to from this day forward?

2. Allowing even 1% chance of not completing the goal can be disastrous. From this day forward I am committing or recommitting 100% to being THE

   _______________________________.

3. Am I willing to die for the truth that I believe in? When I meet my maker and my maker asks what I did with all the talent I was given I will be able to say

   ____

Requirement 7

Edison muffs

An "a" focuses on the wrong
things at the wrong times.
A THE understands the
importance of when to listen
and when not to listen. You
must know how to control this
aspect of your life.

Don't Be An A!

Requirement 7

Edison muffs

Ignore the 20 (to help the 2 million)

Requirement number 7 states you must use your Edison muffs to focus in. Thomas Edison says his partial deafness helped him to focus on his projects. Apply the example as a metaphor to help your ability to focus.

Who in your life is holding you back? Who are you listening to that's giving you bad advice? Do you even realize the advice you're receiving might be harmful?

You know the importance of surrounding yourself with people who will move you forward towards your potential, not hold you back by making it seem like everything is okay. Is it your co-workers, your partners, your family or maybe even one of your friends who is holding you back and you don't even know it?

Why aren't you where you want to be? Are the people around you supportive, motivational (whether negatively or positively) or vindictive and resentful?

You might need to ignore the opinions of the

20 people closest to you so that you can get your blessings out to the millions of people that need to hear it.

Know how to find your zone

Where is your zone? Where is your mental state when everything seems to work smoothly? Do you know how to replicate the process of getting into that precious state of efficiency? How do you do it?

If you cannot repeat, right now, how to get yourself into your most effective mind state then you must go on the quest to find the answer. You must look for the steps that cause you to enter the zone.

In sports, the zone, is referred to the period of time when all your skills are working in proper order without thinking. In the zone you don't think, you just do. If you are thinking, then you are not operating at maximum efficiency.

When it's time for an "a" to perform, they are often thinking their way through the process. An "a" will be on stage giving a performance and be thinking of the crowd, thinking if they look good, thinking if they're talking too slow, too fast or if they are speaking correctly.

You may be thinking that it would make sense to think about those things on stage. You're wrong. An "a" thinks about those things. A THE <u>knows</u> they look good, knows how the crowd is responding, knows if they're talking too slow, too fast or connecting with the crowd.

A THE knows that when it's time to be on stage then it's time to be on stage and not in your head. If you mess up, fine, you can fix it after the performance during practice.

THE's are present in the moment and not worried what people think because they know they're giving their best. The only time to be embarrassed is if you slacked on your preparation, if you skipped out on a few practices or if you didn't take your training as seriously as you could.

You must know how to find your zone and that means knowing how to perform without thinking.

If you're in the middle of a big presentation you must be natural. You cannot be natural if you're thinking about everything that's going on. You must be trained to allow your body and mind to take over. The only way you build this trust is through repetition.

The only way you can ever find the zone is through repetition of preparation.

An "a" trains a little bit and they do a disservice to themselves because, you can never get into the zone if you haven't fully prepared at maximum effort.

Have you been in the zone lately? If you answered no, then the most likely reason is your preparation has not been the best. If you haven't been in the zone it's because you're operating like an "a", and not a THE.

Be detached from the outcome

If you want to be THE then the outcome must not influence your actions. The outcome is a by-product of the work you put in. The outcome only matters to the fans. Your outcomes will take care of themselves because you know how to focus on the details.

What do the weak-minded "a's" focus on? What do the fans, that don't know the work that's put in, focus on? They focus on the outcome because they know of nothing else.

The only reason you care about the outcome is to measure your progress personally and see what you need to work on more. You are stoic and have a mindset that's one of a kind. You are THE!

What happens when your book doesn't sell many copies? Nothing. What happens when your marathon time is slower than last time? Nothing. What happens when you get on stage and nobody laughs at your jokes? Nothing. Nothing happens except you know what you need to work on.

A THE is not distracted by the opinions of others because you know that you'll be back in the ring in a very short time with a better version of yourself.

Be THE by knowing how to focus and what to

Edison Muffs

focus on.
Don't be an A.

Next.

Applying the 7ᵗʰ Requirement:
Edison muffs

1. Who in your life is providing resistance instead of support? Reconfirm the mission you are on and note the people you will be able to help by accomplishing it.

2. Knowing how to find your zone or the steps that lead up to your ability to enter it are key for being THE. What can you do to operate in this state of mind more frequently?

3. Remain detached from the outcome. The outcome, is either a measurement of what areas you can improve or it's someone's opinion of your performance. You remain detached knowing that you continue to improve on yourself.

Requirement 8

In the flow

A THE knows how to find the flow of positive energy and live in it. We are all connected, and you must live in the important conductor of good vibes.

Requirement 8
In the Flow

Tune in – pay attention

The 8th requirement addresses the awareness of the energy you surround yourself with. Are you paying attention to your surroundings? Is your environment made for growth? Are your peers boosting you or burying you?

What material or natural things do you consistently surround yourself with? Are you cohabiting with grandeur such as the ocean, mountains or super high-achievers?

Everything you surround yourself with gives off a certain energy. You know people that can light up a room just by walking into it. And you also know people who can make any room feel like a funeral home as soon as they walk through the door.

What have you been watching on T.V. or the internet in the last week? Have you been watching too much news and not enough inspirational stories? Have you been overly consumed with gossip, sports or tragedies that occur around the world?

What have you been bringing up in conversation over the last week? What have you been talking about around the office? Have you been a catalyst of encouragement or a participator in "a" talk?

Have you been talking about grand ideas or gossiping about people?

A THE talks about ideas or impact whereas an "a" talks about people and injustices in their life.

The energy you put out will be returned. You will attract people into your life with like energy. It is imperative to tune in and self-check your energy.

A THE knows the importance of bringing good vibes and good spirits to a room. You don't have to be silly, goofy or aloof with your positive energy. You must understand that what you do will rub off on others. Be aware.

An "a" is unaware.

Be THE.

Next.

Karma is already done to you

Whatever you put into this world, it comes back to you. If you are putting out good, good will come back to you in some form. If you dump negativity onto the world it comes back to you in some form. But you don't have to worry about dumping negativity because plenty of "a's" are doing enough of that.

You are THE.

You understand that your actions are felt in this world and every single action you take has an impact. Some impacts are larger than others but all are felt.

What karma are you putting into the world? How are you treating the people around you? Are you treating people with respect or do you think you're better than others?

A true THE understands that each person carries the same value as any other human being. You are THE most caring, most respectful, most empathetic.

Wherever you go you leave people in a better place.

What do people say when you walk into the room? What do they say while you're there? What do they say when you leave the room?

Can people feel your energy in the room? If not, why not?

Be the energy source. You are a massively powerful source of energy. You don't do it for others, you do it because that's the way you are. It's not a show, a performance or an act. You are a powerful energy.

You put immense positive realistic energy into the world and you feel it coming back to you. There's no mistaking the good karma that comes your way. It's a by-product of your actions.

You put love into the world and get it back 10-fold. You circulate money into the world and get it back 10-fold. You put excitement, adventure and respect into the world. And you get it all back 10-fold. 100-fold. Heck, 1000-fold.

You are THE. Be THE!

Don't aspire to be, just be

Are you spending too much time aspiring to be something? Are you aspiring to be super healthy, a great student, or financially independent?

STOP aspiring and start BEING!

Stop talking about the thing and start being the thing. Do you want to write a screenplay? Then start writing it. The moment you pick up the pen or touch the keypad you shift from "aspiring" to doing or being.

It's not complicated. Don't complicate it.

Just be it.

Are you worried what people will say? Don't be. Their opinions do not matter. Only "a's" worry about the opinion of others. Only "a's" spend all their time aspiring. Only "a's" use language like "I wish, you're so lucky, must be nice."

You don't aspire to be. You just BE.

Don't aspire to make a difference. Go make a difference.

Don't aspire to write another story. Write the story.

Don't aspire to get in shape. Put this book down right now and do 10 pushups. (Side note: I actually stopped writing to do 10 pushups).

You should not have made it through this chapter without taking some form of action to BE.

"a's" aspire to be and THE's BE.

Are you getting compliments on how much you are accomplishing and how quickly it appears you get things done? Do people constantly ask you how you do it all? Are your actions in line with your thoughts?

Don't think about being something, JUST BE.

Do the thing you need to do to be the person you intend to be.

Don't aspire to be, just BE!

Applying the 8ᵗʰ Requirement:
In the flow

1. How can you be more in-tune with your surroundings? How can you be more intentional about recognizing patterns around you and being non-judgmental?

2. What can you do today to add good karma to your life? What daily habits can you put in place to insure good daily karma? i.e. tipping the coffee barista, holding the door, saying hi to a random person, or giving genuine compliments to people.

3. Listen to your internal dialogue, what is it saying that you aspire to be? What have you been telling yourself that you aspire to be one day? Your job is to BE. What is one step you can take right now to start being and stop aspiring?

Requirement 9

Be THE now

It's a habit thing. Be THE. That's all you need to remember. The requirements are habits, exercises, reminders etc. to keep you pushing yourself forward. These are the supporting cast members of the main attraction. The main attraction is your mindset of being THE and leaving your "A" personality behind you.

Requirement 9

Be THE Now

The hands at the end of your arm

Requirement number 9 states that you have the abilities, now use them.

Look down at your hands. The hands attached to the end of your arms are what you need to get started. Are you waiting for someone to give you a lucky break? Are you waiting for someone to knock on your door and ask for your product? Are you waiting for a celebrity to announce your business to the world?

The only action you need to take at this moment is entirely possible with the two hands at the ends of your arms.

You are the person in control. An "a" waits for help from someone else. An "a" says I need to study more before I take action. An "a" finds excuses to justify their lack of action. What does a THE do? What do you do?

You act. You act with intention and discipline. Your intention is created by the two hands at the end of your arms. You create the opportunities.

You are THE person who gets things done.

What will people say about you when you're

not around? They will say you are a person of action, of decision and of courage with your abilities. They say you are self-reliant.

Your self-reliance gives you power. Your self-reliance is created by the two hands at the ends of your arms. Those two hands set everything else in motion.

Your hands pick up the phone to make the phone calls, they shake the hands of the deals that need made, and they pick up the tools you need to build your life.

What else do you need besides your own hands to get started? You may need other help along the way but to get started all you need is your own hands.

A THE uses what they have. What do you have right now that can be the start or continuation of your bigger intentions? Look around you.

Seriously.

Stop reading this for a second and look at the gifts you have surrounding you.

You probably have a phone near by. A laptop. Pen or pencil and paper. A vehicle. A floor to do push-ups.

Most importantly you have your creativity and ability to think. What else do you need?

It's time to use the hands at the end of your arms and MAKE action.

Be THE!

Next.

See yourself as THE

What does your self-talk sound like? Are you building yourself into the person you desire or allowing negativity to control your actions?

If you don't see yourself as THE then it will be impossible for anyone else to see you that way. And if someone does see you as THE you will sabotage it somehow because you don't believe it yourself.

No rule, law or principle exists stating you will be punished for creating the self-image you desire. You have the ability and must do whatever it takes mentally to believe you are THE.

You must know that you have put the work in and you continue to put the work in. Every day you wake up you are even better than the day before. Everything you do, in the context of your mastery, has a purpose.

You do life on purpose.

Look at the often used, and casually stated phrase of "on purpose". It means you do life purposefully. You have an intention and you know it is manifested daily in your actions.

You know how to get yourself back on track

when you slip.

An "a" finds reasons they cannot be the best. A THE sees everything as the exact reason why they can be the best.

Are you the shortest person in the room? Good, that means you stand out.

Are you the biggest person in the room? Good, that means you stand out.

No matter what the circumstance you have, it's the precise reason why you have what it takes to stand out and BE THE!.

Next.

Make Action

It's time to stop "taking" action and start making action. An "a" is lazy in their language, a THE understands the power in the words they speak.

The term "take action" simply does not make sense. It implies you have to get action from somewhere else.

You don't.

You MAKE action!

A THE thinks differently. And you are a THE!

Look at the definitions.

Take - Defined as an amount of something

gained or **acquired** from one source or in one session.

Now, take a look at the definition of Make.

Make – form something by putting parts together or combining substances, construct, create.

Another definition is: compose, prepare or draw up something

Another definition is: to cause something to exist; bring about

It's absolutely clear that MAKING action is far more empowering than taking action.

Take a moment to visualize yourself in both mindsets.

1) A person that takes action

Or

2) THE person that MAKES action!

What kind of person do you want to be known for? Which type of person would inspire you more? Don't you think you should be the one that changes the game and inspires by MAKING action?

Do we agree?

NO MORE TAKING ACTION.

From this point on in your life you MAKE

ACTION. You're not taking anything anywhere. Where would you "take" action anyways?

You are THE catalyst of action. The melting pot of manifestation.

Your entire being is about creating the outcomes and having the mindset of a master. You don't have to "take" anything from anyone.

You simply create.

MAKE massive action.

How does that mindset feel? How does it sound when you say, "I MAKE action" opposed to "taking" action? Can you see yourself "MAKING" action?

How much more efficient are you with that mindset?

You are a THE. THE maker of action. THE maker of results. THE person of discipline.

You MAKE action.

Applying the 9th Requirement
Make Action

1. You have the helping hand at the end of your arms. What is surrounding your right now that you can utilize to expand your reach, value or service?

2. You have the mindset of a THE that MAKES action. Now you visualize yourself as a person that MAKES action. What is one action you are committed to making in the next five minutes to get you closer to your goals? i.e. send an email, make a phone call, start writing a book etc.

3. BE THE. After all you have reminded yourself in this book the last and most important thing to remember is to keep things simple. The way to keep it simple is to remind yourself daily that your duty is to: Be THE. You are THE. You do not have to wait to be THE. At this very moment when you say it in your mind it is true. Now go prove it to yourself.

CONCLUSION

You now know the requirements for making the shift, from participating like an "a", to leading like a THE.

It's time to pass this knowledge and mindset to the people you surround yourself with. Grow a large team of THE's and you will maximize your potential in life.

Don't wait to become THE leader, start right now and recommit to pursuing your highest ability. Share this with your friends, co-workers, organization or cause.

You have what it takes and I believe in you.

On your way up, don't forget to reach back and pull someone else up with you.

It's time to become THE leader.

Don't be an A!

Be THE.

Do you want to have a **THE** mentality in your business?

Hire Jake to speak at your next event or corporate training.

Send inquiry to

questions@JakeBollig.com

**The following are
a few motivational
quotes from long ago.**

**Cut them out and
place them where
they will catch your
attention.**

"Every great dream
begins with a dreamer.
Always remember, you
have within you the
strength, the patience,
and the passion to reach
for the stars to change
the world."

Harriet Tubman

"**"Man's greatness consists in his ability to do and the proper application of his powers to things needed to be done."**

Frederick Douglass

"I love those who can smile in trouble, who can gather strength from distress, and grow brave by reflection. 'Tis the business of little minds to shrink, but they whose heart is firm, and whose conscious approves their conduct, will pursue their principles unto death."

Leonardo da Vinci

"Each man is good in His sight. It is not necessary for eagles to be crows."

Sitting Bull

"The will to win, the desire to succeed, the urge to reach your full potential... these are the keys that will unlock the door to personal excellence."

Confucius

"There is no great genius without some touch of madness."

Aristotle

"Success in life is
founded upon attention
to the small things rather
than to the large things;
to the every day things
nearest to us rather than
to the things that are
remote and uncommon."

Booker T. Washington

“If I can create the
minimum of my plans
and desires, there shall
be no regrets.”

Bessie Coleman

The following requirement lists serve as a good reminder sheet.

Cut them out and place them strategically in your daily life.

This will provide a good reminder for you to keep pursuing your potential.

<u>9 Requirements:</u>

1. **Compare you to you**

2. **Be a pro**

3. **Fail Big**

4. **Embrace the pain**

5. **Think Universally**

6. **Commit**

7. **Edison muffs**

8. **In the flow**

9. **Be THE now.**

9 Requirements:

1. **Compare you to you**

2. **Be a pro**

3. **Fail Big**

4. **Embrace the pain**

5. **Think Universally**

6. **Commit**

7. **Edison muffs**

8. **In the flow**

9. **Be THE now.**

9 Requirements:

1. **Compare you to you**

2. **Be a pro**

3. **Fail Big**

4. **Embrace the pain**

5. **Think Universally**

6. **Commit**

7. **Edison muffs**

8. **In the flow**

9. **Be THE now.**

If you liked this book, make sure to get Jake's other title:

Gifts From Nicholas

A fast-paced fictional story on how to handle failures.

GiftsFromNicholas.com

Jake Bollig is a leading author, speaker and workshop provider on the psychology of achievement. If your organization needs a boost in morale, a refreshment of vision or a reminder of why they started then ask about Jake's services.

Send your inquiry on speaking fees or questions to questions@jakebollig.com

Products and info at JakeBollig.com

www.ingramcontent.com/pod-product-compliance
Lightning Source LLC
Chambersburg PA
CBHW062150221025